Grace Simpson
(Interlaken / Vitznau
July 2002)

Alfred Pohler

Enchanting
Alpine Flowers

Verlag Lohmann — A-6433 Oetz, Tirol

Front cover:
Valuga Lechtaler Alps
Blue Monkshood and Alpine Ragwort

Back cover:
Martagon Lily in a field in the Komperdell

ISBN 3-85373-035-3

All photographs, descriptions and drawings by the author
English translation: Jacqueline Schweighofer

Edition: 1991
All rights reserved.
Publisher: Verlag Lohmann, A-6433 Oetz, Tirol
Tel. 0 52 52 / 65 78 - Alpina Druck Innsbruck
Printed in Austria

FOREWORD

What would the Alps be without their floral decoration? All that delight at the sight of flower-carpeted meadows and rocks ablaze with colour would be missing. It is a particular gift of the Creator that enables us to comprehend all this enchanting beauty — a glimpse of paradise, as it were.

It is not merely the immeasurable variety and the riotous colour of these delightful specimens that is so fascinating; it is, too, their exemplary and frequently dramatic fight for survival which is so impressive.

The enormous efforts to secure propagation by a wide variety of shapes and by brilliant colours are indications of Nature's inventiveness and her inimitable technique. Even in our modern, highly technical world the pliancy and elasticity of such plant cells is incomparably perfect. Such magnificent feats arouse our boundless admiration.

It was our aim to provide a representative survey of all these colourful creations with their extravagant profusion of bloom. One hundred conspicuously flowering Alpine plants are pictured in colour, accompanied by brief botanical descriptions on the opposite page.

The survey is not arranged in any particular order; the plants are grouped according to colour and are alphabetically ordered. To make identification easier the whole plant is shown; since this can also be misleading, however, the normal height of the stem is given first in the description.

References to the size of flowers and leaves or the thickness of the stem are relative and apply to the particular plant described. Botanical terms are defined in the "Botany in brief" section. Coloured markings down the edge of the pages and the alphabetically ordered index of plants serve to facilitate the search. The book has been designed so as to be easily carried.

In awareness of the protection these exquisite plants require and knowing that they can only fully display their entire splendour in a natural environment, may it be the aim and the responsibility of all to preserve this magnificent world of Alpine flowers for as long as possible.

Reutte, 1985   Alfred Pohler

Biotope on the Pordoijoch with the Langkofel range, South Tyrol

ALPINE ROSE
Rhododendron ferrugineum

Family:	Heather Family Ericaceae
Shrub:	20—100 cm high, ramose, branches round, woody, brown-grey, bare, foliate, hardy
Leaves:	petiolate or sessile, lanceolate-elliptic, entire, green above, shiny, reddish-scaly beneath, young leaves green beneath, alternate, hardy
Flowers:	dense terminal clusters, funnel-shaped corolla — campanulate with five blunt lobes, bright red, a few white stamens, pleasant scent. Calyx 5-merous, pointed, accumbent, green
Flowering time:	June—August
Habitat:	1500—3000 m, calcifuge soils rich in humus, mountain meadows, alpine pastures, heaths, scrubland, open woods, boulder terrain Fairly frequent. Locally prolific

Distribution: Alps, Pyrenees, northern Apennines

CREEPING AZALEA

Loiseleuria procumbens

Family:	Heather Family Ericaceae
Dwarf shrub:	with prostrate, ramose branches, trunk up to 45 cm long, gnarled, woody, round, densely foliate
Leaves:	opposite, small, linear, margins rolled under, dark green, shiny, evergreen
Flowers:	terminal clusters, pink to dark red, 5-merous calyx, corolla light pink, campanulate, 5 lobes, ovate purplish red buds
Flowering time:	May—August
Habitat:	1500—3000 m, avoids lime, overgrown ridges, rocky heaths, morainic slopes, schistose banks, mat-like or forming cushions. Frequent.
Distribution:	Alps

MUSK THISTLE

Carduus nutans

Family: Daisy Family Compositae

Stem: 40—120 cm high, erect, sturdy, branching, green-grey, prickly foliate, shrub-like

Leaves: alternate, sessile, lanceolate, pointed, deeply pinnatifid, lobes irregularly spiny, stiff, leathery, decurrent, green-grey, long

Flowers: solitary terminal flower heads, 3—6 cm in diameter, nodding, disc florets only, purplish red; bracts lanceolate, pointed, spiny, green, turned back in full flower, tinged red

Flowering time: July—September

Habitat: up to 2000 m, stony ground, meadows, scree, scarps, sunny slopes, at edge of woods and thickets, wetlands. Infrequent.

Distribution: Alps, Pyrenees, Norway

MELANCHOLY THISTLE

Cirsium helenioides

Family:	Daisy Family Compositae
Stem:	40—120 cm high, erect, round, fluted, green foliate, tinged red, woolly
Leaves:	large, 20—40 cm long, 4—8 cm wide, toothed, pinnately-lobed, too, with sections turned upwards, white-woolly beneath, matt green above, alternate; top stem leaves narrow-lanceolate, entire, sessile
Flowers:	terminal, on long, vigorous stalks, one to three large flower heads, 3—4 cm in diameter, disc florets only, longer at edge, dark pink to purple; spherical involucre with dark brown scaly flower bracts
Flowering time:	July—August
Habitat:	up to 1700 m, moist soils, low in lime, banks of streams, wet, stony, mountain meadows, slopes, scrub areas, with Alpine roses, head-waters. Infrequent. Rare in calcareous districts.
Distribution:	Alps

VULGAR THISTLE

Cirsium vulgare

Family: Daisy Family Compositae

Stem: 60—120 cm high, bush, usually branching, foliate, spiny winged, green, sturdy

Leaves: alternate, deeply pinnately lobed, spiny, rough, cobwebby woolly beneath, side leaf tip bifid, lanceolate with long, strong spine at end, green, decurrent

Flowers: solitary, terminal, occasionally two to three, large, 3—4 cm in diameter and 6—8 cm long, involucre ovate, disc florets only, dark pink or purple; very small, spiny flower bracts

Flowering time: June—September

Habitat: up to 1800 m, nitrogenous soils, at edge of woods and thickets, wetlands, pastures, stony meadows, clearings, at edge of paths.
Frequent.

Distribution: Alps, Pyrenees, Apennines, throughout Europe

GERMAN GENTIAN

Gentianella germanica

Family:	Gentian Family Gentianaceae
Stem:	5—40 cm high, erect, slender, round, branching, foliate, green-brown
Leaves:	radical, spatulate to widely lanceolate, entire, parallel veined, green; stem leaves ovate-lanceolate, sessile, green, tinged brownish red
Flowers:	dense racemes, five petal lobes, ovate-pointed, violet to pink, more rarely white, throat bearded, calyx funnel-shaped to tubular; sepals lanceolate, pointed, flat, green-brown, petals spreading
Flowering time:	June—October
Habitat:	up to 2800 m, stony, poor soils, warm, stony slopes, mountain meadows, pastures, open moorland. Scattered.

Distribution: Alps

PROTECTED!

SPRING HEATH

Erica herbacea

Family: Heather Family Ericaceae

Stem: dwarf shrub, erect or ascending, thickly branched, twigs woody, slender, round, brown, foliate, up to 35 cm long

Leaves: slim, linear, acicular, sessile, evergreen, leathery, frequently verticillate on twig, 6—7 mm long, bare, pointed

Flowers: long clusters, turned to one side, usually terminal, corolla four-merous, bell-shaped to jug-shaped, pink or purple; sepals four-merous, same colour or darker, fleshy red, eight stamens, one style, flower on short stalk, nodding

Flowering time: February—May

Habitat: 600—2600 m, on stony, sunny soils, warm meadows, rocks, slopes, open woods, dwarf shrub heaths, wetlands, open pine woods.
Frequent, gregarious, cushions.

Distribution: Alps, Apennines, Illyrian Mountains, Jura, Apuan Alps

ORANGE LILY
Lilium bulbiferum

Family: Lily Family Liliaceae

Stem: 20—100 cm high, erect, strong, round, sulcate, green, foliate

Leaves: alternate, lanceolate to linear, entire, hairy, green; bulbils of up to pea-size in the leaf axils

Flowers: terminal, solitary, but up to five large flowers, too, six petals, ovate, pointed, bright orange, erect, frequently brown spotted; protruding stigma and brownish red stamens

Flowering time: June—July

Habitat: 800—1700 m, calcareous soils, screes, boulders, sunny mountain meadows, pastures, slopes.
Rare, completely absent in many areas.

Distribution: Alps (particularly Dolomites, southern Alps, maritime Alps, northern limestone Alps)

PROTECTED!

CENTAUREA SCABIOSA

Family:	Daisy Family Compositae
Stem:	20—80 cm high, erect, sturdy, ramose, round-sulcate, green, foliate
Leaves:	alternate, sessile, pinnate, deeply notched, single lobes oblong-linear, pointed, green; lower stem leaves with short stalks, shiny
Flowers:	large, spherical heads, disc florets pink-violet to purple, marginal petals larger, pinnately split; spherical calyx, dense, widely lanceolate flower bracts, brown, villous
Flowering time:	July—September
Habitat:	800—2400 m, various soils, meadows, edge of paths, pastures, with pines, slopes. Infrequent. Gregarious, locally profuse.
Distribution:	Alps, Apennines, Pyrenees

CENTAUREA RHAPONTICA

Family: Daisy Family Compositae

Stem: 35—110 high, erect, sturdy, thickening towards flower, sulcate, green, downy, foliate

Leaves: radical, stalked, large, up to 50 cm long and 12 cm wide, ovate-lanceolate, dentate, grey downy beneath; stalk leaves alternate, somewhat smaller, ovate-lanceolate, lobate, margined, sessile or encircling stalk, reticulate, grey-downy beneath

Flowers: terminal, solitary, large, 5—11 cm in diameter, disc florets only, dark pink to purple; spherical involucre, flower bracts rounded, inflated, accumbent, light brown

Flowering time: July—September

Habitat: 1500—2500 m, predominantly on silicate soils, boulder slopes, scrubby places, wet, stony meadows, windless, warm slopes.
Somewhat rare.
Locally prolific.

Distribution: Alps (southern Alps, Julian Alps)

CENTAUREA JACEA

Family:	Daisy Family Compositae
Stem:	15—60 cm high, erect, hardly branched, slender, foliate, round, rarely angular, hairy, green
Leaves:	alternate, pinnatifid, oblong to lance-olate, tapering at stalk; upper stem leaves usually undivided, entire, lanceolate, green
Flowers:	solitary, terminal, 25—50 mm diameter, disc florets only, marginal petals larger, pink to reddish violet; outer bracts brown with scaly, brownish appendages
Flowering time:	June—September
Habitat:	up to 1600 m, wet and dry soils, poor grass, meadows, mountain pastures, moorland, edge of paths. Common, widespread, usually prolific.
Distribution:	Alps, Pyrenees, Norway

ALPINE HOUSELEEEK

Sempervivum alpinum

Family: Stonecrop Family Crassulaceae

Stem: 10—40 cm high, erect, foliate, glandular hairs

Leaves: rosettes up to 8 cm in diameter, leaves fat, fleshy, green with bluish shimmer, ciliate, brownish red prickly tip; erect on the stem, tinged red

Flowers: branching pistil, several florets with large corollas, pink to pale red, darker stripes, lanceolate petals, erect stamens, purple style

Flowering time: July to September

Habitat: 1200—2400 m, basic to acid soils, overgrown detritus, rocky shelves, crevices, steep meadows

Distribution: Lechtal Alps

MOUNTAIN HOUSELEEK

Sempervivum montanum

Family: Stonecrop Family Crassulaceae

Stem: 5—20 cm high, erect, round, sturdy, green to reddish brown, foliate

Leaves: small spherical rosettes, tiny, round, succulent, light green leaves with short red tip, glandular hairs; stem leaves lanceolate, succulent, greenish yellow, red tinged, red tips, accumbent, decurrent, scaly on stem

Flowers: one to three terminal, 2—3 cm diameter, 12 to 16 petals, linear to lanceolate, forming a star, purple to violet red, lighter at edge, numerous stamens, ovary and style lemon yellow

Flowering time: July—September

Habitat: 1800—3200 m, calcifuge, on silicate rock, stony mountain meadows, dwarf shrub heaths, ridges, boulder areas, screes.
Common.

Distribution: Alps, Pyrenees, Carpathians

PROTECTED!

COBWEB HOUSELEEK

Sempervivum arachnoideum

Family: Stonecrop Family Crassulaceae

Stem: 4—25 cm high, erect, sturdy, green or brownish red, scaly leaved

Leaves: ground rosettes, spatulate or ovate, pointed, green, frequently tinged red, cobweb of hairs between the leaves; stem leaves alternate, lanceolate, blunt, fleshy, accumbent, green or brownish red

Flowers: usually several in a terminal cyme, corolla approx. 20 mm in diameter, single petals widely lanceolate, pointed, forming a star, red to reddish violet; stamens upright, purple, yellow pollen at top

Flowering time: July—September

Habitat: 1700—3200 m, calcareous and acid soils, crevices, bouldered slopes, rocks. Somewhat rare.

Distribution: Alps, Apennines, Pyrenees

PROTECTED!

34

ALPINE BELLS
Cortusa matthioli

Family:	Primrose Family Primulaceae
Stem:	15—25 cm high, erect or ascending, slender, round, green, leafless
Leaves:	radical, large, stalked, rounded, lobed, crenate, ribbed, hairy, green
Flowers:	several flowers, hanging umbel, corolla funnel to bell-shaped, five petals, ovate, dark red to purple, nodding, stalked; sepals slit deeply, green, prominent, hairy
Flowering time:	July—August
Habitat:	1100—1800 m, nutritious soils, damp places, rocks, banks of streams, scrubland, semi-shade. Infrequent.
Distribution:	Alps

AUTUMN CROCUS

Colchicum autumnale

Family:	Lily Family Liliaceae
Stemless!	6 petals on an elongated tube (mock stem), whitish below, pink tinged above, round, 8—15 cm high
Leaves:	3 radical, large, widely lanceolate, fleshy, deep green, shiny, tulip-like, leafless when in flower! Leaves appear in the spring, in the centre 3-merous capsule on sturdy stalk
Flowers:	solitary, tulip-like, 6 petals forming a funnel-shaped calyx, non-coalescent section 3—7 cm long, elliptic-lance-olate, long, pink to mauve, entire, margined, 3 white styles, 6 golden stamens. Leafless in autumn at flowering time, leaves appear in following spring.
Flowering time:	August—October
Habitat:	up to 2200 m, likes nitrogen, clay soil, damp meadows
Distribution:	Alps, Pyrenees, Apennines

POISONOUS! COMMON!

SOLDIER or MILITARY ORCHID

Orchis militaris

Family: Orchid Family Orchidaceae

Stem: 20—50 cm high, erect, strong, bare, green, tinged brownish red above, round to slightly angular

Leaves: radical, oblong-elliptic, thickish, sheath-like at base, green, shiny, bracts short, pointed, membranous

Flowers: dense, pyramid-shaped or oblong spikes, florets stalked, the five upper petals forming a close helmet, pale pink outside, darker stripes inside, outer sepals pointed, inner sepals linear-pointed, somewhat shorter than the outer sepals; lip narrow, three lobes, light red with purple markings; side lobes narrow-linear, central lobe divided into two points with a small tail in between, spur down-curved

Flowering time: May—June

Habitat: up to 1800 m, calcareous, dry soils, damp marshy ground, meadows with poor soil, clearings, edge of woods and bushes, slopes

Distribution: Alps, Apennines, Pyrenees

PROTECTED!

EARLY PURPLE ORCHID

Orchis mascula

Family:	Orchid Family Orchidaceae
Stem:	20—60 cm high, erect, sturdy, round, green-brown, foliate, bare, not branching, usually hollow
Leaves:	radical, wide-lanceolate, keeled, slightly fleshy, green, unspotted; stem leaves alternate, lanceolate, decurrent, parallel veined, bracts lanceolate, accumbent, violet red
Flowers:	spikes, single flowers 12—15 mm long, sepals curved, margin wavy, turned up, petals inclined, 3-lobed lip, violet-red or light pink, spur horizontal or up-curved, same length as ovary
Flowering time:	May—August
Habitat:	800—1800 m, calcareous and acid soils, stony meadows, pastures, wetlands, marshy ground, mountain fields. Infrequent.
Distribution:	Alps, Apennines, Pyrenees

PROTECTED!

BLACK VANILLA ORCHID

Nigritella nigra

Family: Orchid Family Orchidaceae

Stem: 5—20 cm high, erect, round, slightly sulcate, green, slender, foliate

Leaves: linear-lanceolate, grooved, pointed, grass-like, green, entire; stem leaves lanceolate, very pointed, sessile or decurrent, green, accumbent

Flowers: pyramid-shaped, round, densely flowered heads (shorter than rosy vanilla orchid), single flowers brown to dark wine red, narrow, spreading perianth lobes, lip pointing upwards, tapering at base, spur short, sturdy, pleasantly scented

Flowering time: June—August

Habitat: 1400—2400 m, warm, sunny mountain meadows, alps, pastures, overgrown ridges.
Infrequent. Gregarious.

Distribution: Alps, Apennines, Pyrenees, Norway

KERNER'S LOUSEWORT

Pedicularis kerneri

Family: Figwort Family Scrophulariaceae

Stem: 5—15 cm, curved upwards, slender, green, red tinged, hairy, few leaves, unbranching shoots

Leaves: radical, stalked, linear-lanceolate, green, singly pinnate, short teeth, frequently tinged reddish brown or purple, round

Flowers: few in loose clusters from top leaf axils, large corolla, approx. 20 mm diameter, five-merous, pink to light purple; upper lip somewhat darker, turning upwards, cut off at top, beak-like, lower lip bare, entire; calyx tubular, brownish red, with small, pointed tips

Flowering time: June—September

Habitat: 1800—3200 m, lime-deficient, siliceous rock, mountain meadows, overgrown ridges, strips of rock, screes, stony pastures.
Infrequent.

Distribution: Alps, Pyrenees (central Alps from Salzburg to west Alps)

MOSS CAMPION

Silene acaulis

Family: Pink Family Caryophyllaceae

Stem: very short, not branching, forming flat cushions, densely crowded, slender stalks, round, green, foliate

Leaves: opposite, small, narrow-lanceolate, pointed, numerous, green ciliate

Flowers: terminal, solitary, 6—10 mm diameter, five petals, ovate-long, blunt slightly notched, pink to purple, throat whitish with yellow stamens, sometimes forming large, flat cushions

Flowering times: June—August

Habitat: 1600—3200 m, overgrown, stony soils, grassy ledges of rock, mountain ridges, warm, sunny mountain pastures, boulders.
Quite frequent.

Distribution: Alps, Apennines, Pyrenees, Norway

PROTECTED!

MARTAGON LILY

Lilium martagon

Family:	Lily Family Liliaceae
Stem:	30—100 cm high, erect, sturdy, round, green, foliate
Leaves:	verticillate, oblong to wide-lanceolate, deep green, parallel veined; upper stem leaves alternate, too, small, lance-olate-pointed, green
Flowers:	loose cluster, stalked, pendulous, perianth petals long lanceolate, recurved giving turk's cap appearance, pink-purple, brownish red spots; long, curved filaments with ochre-coloured stamens around the style; heavily scented at night
Flowering time:	July—August
Habitat:	1400—2200 m, calcareous soils, mountain meadows, overgrown screes, pastures, edge of woods Infrequent.
Distribution:	Alps, Pyrenees, Apennines

ALPINE ROCK—JASMINE

Androsace alpina

Family:	Primrose Family Primulaceae
Dwarf bush:	forming small, loose cushions or flat mats, stalks 2—5 cm high, round, green, foliate
Leaves:	rosette-like on the stalks, 2—8 cm long, lanceolate to linear, green, densely grouped, starry hairs, pubescent
Flowers:	on short stalks, corolla 7—9 mm in diameter, five obovate petals, pink to white with yellow throat, single flowers, terminal
Flowering time:	July—August
Habitat:	2200—4200 m, on wet siliceous and shaly rocks, moraines, ridges. Somewhat rare, small amounts locally, completely absent in some areas.
Distribution:	Alps

PROTECTED!

MUSK—MALLOW

Malva moschata

Stem: 30—100 cm high, erect, branching, round, green, foliate, sometimes bush-like with many stems, hairy

Leaves: few on the stem, alternate, short stalked, palmate, five-merous with narrow, pinnate lobes, dentate, green, hairy, sessile at top

Flowers: one to three, terminal or springing from leaf axils of upper stem leaves, large, 4—6 cm in diameter, five petals inversely cordate, straight or notched, pink or white, spreading; numerous prominent stamens, light pink, strong musk scent

Flowering time: July—September

Habitat: up to 1200 m, nutritious soils, deficient in lime, warm slopes, meadows, pastures, river banks.
Somewhat rare, gregarious.

Distribution: Alps, southern Scandinavia

ALPINE PINK

Dianthus alpinus

Family: Pink Family Caryophyllaceae

Stem: 5—15 cm high, erect, slender, round, bare, green, foliate, forming cushions or loose patches

Leaves: opposite, lanceolate-linear, 10—20 mm long, 3—5 mm wide, sessile, green, entire, shiny above; rosette leaves linear, blunt, different lengths

Flowers: terminal, solitary, large, 20—30 mm in diameter, five petals, inversely cordate, dentate, purple, spreading, pink with darker spots towards the throat; calyx with brownish red scales towards the base, otherwise bare

Flowering time: June—August

Habitat: 900—2400 m, calcareous and rich soils, warm, stony mountain meadows, overgrown ridges.
Not frequent, completely absent in parts.

Distribution: Alps (northern and southern limestone chains of the eastern Alps)

PROTECTED!

CARTHUSIAN PINK

Dianthus carthusianorum

Family: Pink Family Caryophyllaceae

Stem: 10—40 cm high, erect, slender, round, green, bare, frequently only one pair of leaves

Leaves: radical, long, linear, pointed, slightly carinate, entire, rough, green

Flowers: clusters of several heads, flower diameter 12—20 mm, petals obovate, notched, pink to purple, calyx conical-tubular to bell-shaped green to purplish brown, calyx scales dark brown, accumbent

Flowering time: June—August

Habitat: 800—2800 m, calcareous and neutral soils, meadows, edge of paths, pastures, strips of rock, ridges and overgrown knolls, mountain fields.
Not frequent, gregarious.

Distribution: Alps, Apennines, Pyrenees

PROTECTED!

FLY ORCHID

Ophrys insectifera

Family:	Orchid Family Orchidaceae
Stem:	15—35 cm high, erect, round, bare, green, foliate
Leaves:	radical, oblong-ovate, parallel veined, keeled, somewhat fleshy, entire, green; stem leaves oblong-ovate to lanceolate, keeled, light green
Flowers:	loose raceme with a few florets, florets stalked, nodding, three perigon petals, turned outwards, lanceolate, green, lower lip 10—15 mm long, fly-like with eyes and feelers and fly-like shape, velvety hairs, reddish brown, central bluish zone, deeply lobed, slightly margined
Flowering time:	April—June
Habitat:	800—1700 m, calcareous, poor soils, stony mountain meadows, pastures, often together with lily of the valley. Very rare.
Distribution:	Alps

PROTECTED!

PAEONY
Paeonia officinalis

Family: Paeony Family Paeoniaceae

Stem: 50—90 cm high, erect or ascending, round, strong, green, bare, foliate, not branching

Leaves: very large, up to 30 cm long, up to 20 cm wide, trifoliate, deeply cut, multiple pinnate sections, lobes lanceolate or oblong-ovate, pointed, green above, grey green beneath, entire, hairy, stalked

Flowers: solitary, terminal, up to 8 cm in diameter, five to eight large petals, bright pink or deep red, wide-ovate to spherical, obtuse, numerous stamens, golden yellow; sepals lanceolate, pointed, spreading, turning out, green or red

Flowering time: May—June

Habitat: up to 1800 m, on limestone or dolomite rock, stony meadows, warm pastures, by oak bushes, dry slopes, frequently together with broom.
Rare, only found in a few areas.

Distribution: Alps, central Apennines (southern Alps, only isolated in the northern Alps)

VILLOUS PRIMROSE

Primula hirsuta

Family:	Primrose Family Primulaceae
Stem:	2—7 cm high, erect or pendulous, round, green, foliate, glandular hairs
Leaves:	ground rosettes, obovate to round, slightly notched, fleshy; glandular hairs
Flowers:	short stalked, umbel-like clusters, single flowers 12—20 mm in diameter, five petals, inversely cordate, some lobes entire, bright pink, flat spreading, whitish eye; calyx bell-shaped, five-merous, accumbent, green
Flowering time:	May—June
Habitat:	1200—3200 m, siliceous and shaly rocks, ridges, damp valleys. Rare, locally prolific.
Distribution:	Alps, Pyrenees

BIRDSEYE PRIMROSE

Primula farinosa

Family: Primrose Family Primulaceae

Stem: 5—25 cm high, erect, round, slender, green, leafless, slightly pubescent

Leaves: ground rosettes, oblong, obovate, crenate, green, bare above, mealy white underneath

Flowers: several in an umbel, corolla 10—20 mm in diameter, five petals, cordate, two lobes, lilac pink to light purple, yellow eye; calyx short, green, mealy, strongly scented

Flowering time: May—August

Habitat: 700—2600 m, various soils, wetlands, meadows, poor pastures, rocky strips, marshes.
Fairly frequent, gregarious.

Distribution: Alps, Pyrenees

SPECTACULAR PRIMROSE
Primula spectabilis

Family: Primrose Family Primulaceae

Stem: 5—12 cm high, erect, round, bare, green

Leaves: radical, oblong-ovate, 6—9 cm long, 2—4 cm wide, bright green, shiny, horny edge, entire

Flowers: in a loose umbel, corolla 20—25 mm diameter, five petals, deeply notched, pink, throat whitish or light pink, calyx tube 8—12 mm long, five sepals, narrow-lanceolate, accumbent, green

Flowering time: May—August

Habitat: 700—2200 m, calcareous soils and those rich in humus, warm, shady pastures, mountain meadows, strips of rock.
Rare, large groups locally.

Distribution: Alps (meadows and rocky areas around Lake Garda), southern Alps

---

PROTECTED!

ROCK SOAPWORT

Saponaria ocymoides

Family:	Pink Family Caryophyllaceae
Stem:	10—40 cm long, creeping, pendulous or ascending, cushion-forming, branching, round, reddish brown, hairy, foliate
Leaves:	obovate, tapering towards leaf stalk, dark green, hairy
Flowers:	panicles of many flowers, corolla 12—15 mm diameter, petals obovate, entire, pink; tubular calyx, brownish red, glandular hairs, sticky
Flowering time:	May—September
Habitat:	800—2000 m, soils deficient in lime, edge of paths, screes, rocks, warm slopes. Infrequent.
Distribution:	Alps

MEZEREON

Daphne mezereum

Family:	Daphne Family Thymelaeaceae
Stem:	20—140 cm high, erect shrub, branching, woody, rarely foliate when in flower
Leaves:	usually near the flower, inversely lanceolate, green, terminal clusters
Flowers:	clusters of 3 flowers, corolla with 4 petals, calyx short, pink; strong pleasant scent
Fruits:	bright red berries, some the size of a pea, arranged in spikes at end of branch
Flowering time:	February—August according to altitude, immediately after snow melts
Habitat:	up to 2700 m, mixed soils, edge of streams, open woodland, wetlands, hedges, bushes, pastures, boulders
Distribution:	Alps

ALPINE SAINFOIN

Hedysarum hedysaroides

Family:	Pea Family Leguminosae
Stem:	10—30 cm high, erect or ascending, not branching, green
Leaves:	unevenly pinnate, five to ten pairs of leaves and end leaf, oblong-elliptical, up to 3 cm long, dark above, light green beneath
Flowers:	one-sided, terminal clusters, up to 40 papilionaceous flowers, purple to reddish violet, arranged like roof tiles, spatulate standard, flowering from bottom to top
Flowering time:	July—August
Habitat:	1600—2800 m, richly calcareous soils, mountain meadows, overgrown screes, rocks, detritus, steep slopes. Infrequent.
Distribution:	Alps, Pyrenees, Carpathians, Caucasus
Note:	Alpine sainfoin is frequently confused with mountain sainfoin (Onobrychis montana or saxatilis.) Features of mountain sainfoin: upright petals, pink, darker veins, less flowers on one spike.

PURPLE SAXIFRAGE
Saxifraga oppositifolia

Family: Saxifrage Family Saxifragaceae

Stem: 5—20 mm high, ascending from trailing shoots, round, slender, branching, sometimes cushion-like, green or brown, foliate

Leaves: rosettes, very small, ovately pointed, green; stem leaves opposite, narrow-ovate to oval, pointed, grey-green, ciliate, entire

Flowers: terminal, solitary, 8—12 mm diameter, five petals, wide-oval or ovate, entire, dark pink to light wine red; calyx bell-shaped, red, sepals small, accumbent, green; stamens purple on brownish stalk, style golden yellow

Flowering time: June—August

Habitat: 1800—3800 m, calcareous and siliceous rocks, crevices, ridges, moraines, screes.
Rather rare.

Distribution: Alps, Apennines, Pyrenees, Norway

PROTECTED!

CENTAURIUM MINUS

Family: Gentian Family Gentianaceae

Stem: 10—35 cm high, erect, square, foliate, branching near inflorescence, green

Leaves: radical, lanceolate, pointed, small, entire; stem leaves oblong-oval, five veined, sessile, green

Flowers: loose cyme, five petals ovate-narrow, spreading, pink, 8—10 mm long, petal tube 8—15 mm long, stamens short, yellow

Flowering time: July—September

Habitat: up to 1200 m, sunny, warm mountain meadows, pastures, semi-dry turf, open woods.
Scattered, entirely absent in places.

Distribution: Alps, Pyrenees

DEVIL'S CLAW

Physoplexis comosa

Family:	Bellflower Family Campanulaceae
Stem:	3—15 cm long, usually hanging, round, slender, foliate, green, more rarely erect or ascending
Leaves:	rosettes, lanceolate to spatulate, coarsely serrate, stalked, green, 4—10 cm long, 1.5—3 cm wide; stem leaves wide-lanceolate, tapering into the stalk, unevenly serrate, green, shiny, 5—10 cm long, 2—3 cm wide
Flowers:	up to 20 long florets forming a cyme, florets stalked, inflated base, tubular towards the top, conically tapering, long point with curved spur, light pink to light violet; tip dark violet to brownish red, two styles with spirally curved stigmas protruding from the conical spurs
Flowering time:	July—August (September)
Habitat:	up to 2700 m, on limestone and dolomite rock, tiny crevices, rocky ledges, boulders. Rare.

Distribution: Alps (southern Alps, Dolomites)

PROTECTED!

ROSEBAY WILLOWHERB

Epilobium angustifolium

Family:	Willowherb Family Onagraceae
Stem:	50—150 cm high, erect, round, slender, light green, foliate, not branching
Leaves:	alternate, sessile, narrow-lanceolate, 6—12 cm long, entire, wavy margin, green, bare
Flowers:	long, single panicles, corolla 1.5—2.5 cm diameter, four short, spatulate, pink or purplish red petals; stigma four-lobed, stamens yellow, stalked, sepals narrow lanceolate, same colour
Flowering time:	July—October
Habitat:	800—2600 m, calcareous and siliceous rock, screes, stony meadows, clearings, banks of streams, embankments, wetlands, open pine woods. Frequent, gregarious.
Distribution:	Alps, Apennines, Pyrenees

Meadow of Alpine flowers, Furgler, Komperdell, Tyrol

PULSATILLA APIIFOLIA

Family:	Buttercup Family Ranunculaceae
Stem:	15—40 cm high, upright, sturdy, round, green-brown, hairy, foliate
Leaves:	radical, stalked, three-merous, pinnate sessile up two thirds of stem, hairy
Flowers:	terminal, solitary, very large, 50—60 mm diameter, usually six petals, ovate, pale yellow, delicate violet outside, slightly hairy; numerous stamens, pale yellow; fruit: bearded tuft of many woolly styles (winged)
Flowering time:	May—July
Habitat:	1700—3000 m, mainly siliceous and shaly soils, mountain meadows, screes, overgrown ridges. Rare, prolific locally.
Distribution:	Alps

PROTECTED!

ARNICA
Arnica montana

Family: Daisy Family Compositae

Stem: 20—55 cm high, erect, round, green, slightly brownish above, hairy, foliate, frequently branching above

Leaves: ground rosette, usually four leaves, oblong, entire, parallel veined, hairy, light green; stem leaves usually two pairs, opposite, ovate sessile, top leaves lanceolate, pointed, opposite, green

Flowers: terminal heads, sometimes several on short stalks, 5—7 cm diameter, disc florets inside, ray florets outside, long, linear, blunt ends, bright yellow; ovary short, cylindrical, green, hairy, strong scent, flower bracts lanceolate, pointed

**Flowering
time:**   June—August

Habitat: 800—2500 m, calcareous and marly soils, acid, marshy meadows, heaths, pastures, clearings, high altitude pastures, mountain fields

Distribution: Alps, northern Apennines, Pyrenees

AURICULA or BEARS—EAR

Primula auricula

Family:	Primrose Family Primulaceae
Stem:	5—25 cm high, erect, round, sturdy, hollow, leafless, green, mealy white
Leaves:	ground rosette, obovate, entire, green, fleshy, mealy powder
Flowers:	terminal umbel of many flowers, individual flowers funnel-shaped, corolla spreading, five petals, ovate-roundish, slightly indented, golden yellow, white throat, nodding, mealy, pleasantly scented
Flowering time:	April—June
Habitat:	900—2600 m, calcareous, dolomitic and siliceous soils, rocks, stony mountain meadows, rocky ridges, gorges. Fairly frequent.
Distribution:	Alps, Apennines

PROTECTED!

SPINIEST THISTLE

Cirsium spinosissimum

Family:	Daisy Family Compositae
Stem:	20—70 cm high, erect or ascending, herbaceous, sometimes branching, frequently several growing from one root
Leaves:	alternate, sessile, large, sinuate, spiny, toothed, green-yellow, lower leaves grass green; sepals yellow-green, pinnately lobed, sharp spines, toothed, hairy, curling
Flowers:	several terminal heads, disc florets only, yellowish white, later yellow-brown, surrounded by toothed, spiny, yellowish green bracts, bracts long, pointed, ascending, spreading in sun
Flowering time:	July—September
Habitat:	1500—2800 m, nutritious loamy soils, fine detritus, mountain pastures, screes, snowy valleys
Distribution:	Alps

YELLOW GENIPI

Artemisia mutellina

Family: Daisy Family Compositae

Stem: 8—25 cm high, erect or ascending, few leaves, silky hairs, slender, reddish brown to greyish green, several from one root

Leaves: stalked, digitately lobed, up to five finger-like leaflets, silky hairs, silvery-shiny, stalked, intensive wormwood smell

Flowers: spherical heads, upright, panicles or spikes, golden yellow, flower bracts silvery glistening, downy, flowerheads approx. 5—6 mm diameter

Flowering time: July—September

Habitat: 1700—3600 m, calcareous, shaly and siliceous rocks, crevices, frequently as exposed as edelweiss; not infrequently found together with wood pinks and edelweiss.
Rare.

Distribution: Alps, Pyrenees, northern Apennines

ENTIRELY PROTECTED!

GREAT YELLOW GENTIAN
Gentiana lutea

Family: Gentian Family Gentianaceae

Stem: 30—130 cm high, upright, strong, round, hollow, green, foliate

Leaves: opposite, ovate, wide, pointed, very large, entire, parallel veined, green, considerably smaller towards end of stem

Flowers: up to ten in terminal end clusters and at leaf axils, petals long-lanceolate, golden yellow, short stalked

Flowering time: July—August

Habitat: 1100—2500 m, mainly calcareous soils, mountain meadows, overgrown screes, pastures, slopes

Distribution: Alps, Apennines

PROTECTED!

SPOTTED GENTIAN

Gentiana punctata

Family: Gentian Family Gentianaceae

Stem: 25—60 cm high, erect, round, strong, green-yellow, foliate

Leaves: opposite, stalked, ovate-elliptic, pointed, very large, parallel veined, green; upper stem leaves more lanceolate, sessile

Flowers: terminal and in clusters at upper leaf axils, erect; flowers large, bell-shaped, five to seven petals, pointed, dullish pale yellow, grey-brown spotted; sepals accumbent, bell-shaped, green

Flowering time: July—September

Habitat: 1500—2800 m, calcareous and siliceous soils, mountain meadows, pastures, stony places, alpine turf. Quite frequent.

Distribution: Alps

PROTECTED!

LAMARCK'S WOLFSBANE

Aconitum lamarckii

Family: Buttercup Family Ranunculaceae

Stem: 50—140 cm high, erect, round, some-times angular, slender, green, hairy, foli-ate, usually several from one root

Leaves: radical, long-stalked, palmate, deeply cut, some pinnate, green, hairy; stem leaves sessile, palmate, five to seven segments with rhomboid sections, smaller towards end of stem

Flowers: loose racemes or on little branches, florets stalked, conspicuously high hel-met, 25—40 mm long, slender, nod-ding, pale cloudy yellow

Flowering time: July—August

Habitat: 1400—2400 m, calcareous, stony soils, screes, avalanche lines, mountain fields, boulders, overgrown ridges, edge of woods, clearings.
Quite frequent, prolific in parts.

Distribution: Alps, Apennines, Pyrenees, Jura

PROTECTED! POISONOUS!

GIANT CATSEAR

Hypochoeris uniflora

Family: Daisy Family Compositae

Stem: 10—50 cm high, erect, round, very strong, thickening towards the flower-head, green; stiff hairs

Flowers: terminal, single heads, 30—50 mm diameter, ray florets long, linear, straight or slightly toothed, golden yellow; calyx in a head, small flower bracts, dark green, stiff hairs, bright, conspicuous plant

Flowering time: July—August

Habitat: 1400—2500 m, poor, warm soils, mountain meadows, pastures, heathery moors, Alpine rose sites. Scattered.

Distribution: Alps, Carpathians

LARGE YELLOW FOXGLOVE

Digitalis grandiflora

Family: Figwort Family Scrophulariaceae

Stem: 25—100 cm high, erect, very strong, round, green, foliate, hairy

Leaves: alternate, wide-lanceolate, sessile, slightly toothed, pronounced venation, green; fluffy hairs beneath

Flowers: in a dense spike on one side, tubular bells, 30—40 mm long, short stalks, five points, lower lip three-lobed, lemon yellow, dotted brown inside, calyx slightly flattened, edge of corolla turning back, hairy, nodding

Flowering time: July—September

Habitat: 1100—1800 m, calcareous and siliceous rock, warm mountain meadows, edge of fir woods, sunny slopes, clearings, boulders.
Not frequent, locally prolific.

Distribution: Alps, Pyrenees

PROTECTED!

105

POTENTILLA RECTA

Family: Rose Family Rosaceae

Stem: 20—60 cm high, erect, several from one root, branching above, round, green-brown, hairy, foliate

Leaves: radical leaves long-stalked, five to seven, serrate, green, hairy; stem leaves alternate, usually seven-merous, deeply serrate; bristly hairs

Flowers: on long stalks, terminal, approx. 2—3 cm in diameter, five petals, heart-shaped, pale yellow, short stamens in centre somewhat darker yellow, inflorescence on main stem in loose panicle with many buds, flower only spreading in warm, sunny weather

Flowering time: June—July

Habitat: up to 1200 m, edge of paths, poor turf, dry, warm slopes, gravel pits, edge of bushes and woods.
Gregarious, scattered to rare.

Distribution: Alps, Apennines, Pyrenees

LADY'S SLIPPER ORCHID

Cypripedium calceolus

Family: Orchid Family Orchidaceae

Stem: 20—60 cm high, erect, strong, round, bare, green, foliate

Leaves: stem leaves, large, widely lanceolate, strong, parallel veined, entire, some margined, encircling stalk and decurrent, deep green, topmost leaves smaller, pointed and usually ribbed lengthways

Flowers: on short, curved stalks emerging at stipule, usually one to three flowers turning to one side; four pointed, twisted, purplish brown petals, very large lip, resembling a clog, 3—5 cm long, hollow, golden yellow, lightly veined in brown, purple spotted nectary at base of lip

Flowering time: May—July

Habitat: 900—1500 m, calcareous, loamy soils, semi-shaded; edge of bushes and woods, open coniferous forests, gorges, banks of streams, slopes, pines

Distribution: Alps, Pyrenees, Norway

Note: the loveliest and most precious local orchid!

PROTECTED!

LARGE FLOWERED LEOPARDSBANE

Doronicum grandiflorum

Family:	Daisy Family Compositae
Stem:	20—60 cm high, erect, round, hollow, green, glandular, hairy, foliate
Leaves:	radical, stalked, large, widely lance-olate, sinuately toothed, green, hairy; stem leaves sometimes sessile or stalked, serrate
Flowers:	terminal, soliatary, very large (3—6 cm diameter) ray florets, linear, golden yellow; disc florets clustered in centre, golden yellow; sepals lanceolate, green, hairy
Flowering time:	July—September
Habitat:	1700—2800 m, loamy, poor soils, screes, pastures, edge of streams, bouldery slopes. Quite frequent.
Distribution:	Alps

YELLOW BELLFLOWER

Campanula thyrsoidea

Family: Bellflower Family Campanulaceae

Stem: 10—50 cm high, erect, very strong, round, green-brown, foliate, bristly hairs

Leaves: alternate, sessile, oblong linear, entire, wavy, green with lighter central vein, hairy; upper leaves narrower, linear, somewhat longer than the flowers, pointed

Flowers: dense cylindrical spike, cup to bell-shaped flowers, 20—40 mm long, pale yellow, slightly upright, long pistil and few stamens, green-yellow

Flowering time: June—August

Habitat: 1500—2500 m, calcareous and siliceous soils, sunny mountain meadows, warm slopes.
Not frequent. Few areas in which it is prolific.

Distribution: Alps

WHITISH HAWKWEED

Hieracium intybaceum All.

Family: Daisy Family Compositae

Stem: 8—20 cm high, erect, one or more heads, glandular hairs, green, thickening towards flowerhead, foliate

Leaves: rosettes, long-lanceolate, coarsely serrate, slightly folded downwards, sticky glandular hairs, green, bracts linear, opposite, glandular

Flowers: terminal, large flowerheads, 3—5 cm diameter, yellowish white, ray florets blunt toothed at end

Flowering time: July—August

Habitat: 1800—2700 m, stony soils, overgrown pastures, meadows, rocky detritus, rocky regions.
Not frequent, scattered.

Distribution: Alps (western Alps, southern Alps, northern limestone Alps)

Note: Hieracium intybaceum has beautifully bright flowers in Alpine terrain, involucre of ray florets little contrast. Alpine plant, rarely subalpine.

WULFEN'S HOUSELEEK

Sempervivum wulfenii

Family:	Stonecrop Family Crassulaceae
Stem:	10—25 cm high, erect or ascending in an arc, round, strong, scaly, foliate, yellow-green
Leaves:	large rosettes, ovate-pointed, succulent, with glandular hairs, green, tips tinged red; stem leaves alternate, lanceolately pointed, sessile, decurrent, yellow to green, accumbent
Flowers:	heads at the end of the stem, flower consisting of 10—18 petals, linear-pointed, spreading in a star, golden yellow, with glandular hairs; numerous stamens, purple, style yellow to green
Flowering time:	July—September
Habitat:	1700—2600 m, calcifuge, siliceous rock, sunny meadows, boulders, rocky ridges. Not frequent, prolific locally.
Distribution:	Alps (predominantly main Alpine ridge)

PROTECTED!

ALPINE POPPY

Papaver alpinum

Family:	Poppy Family Papaveraceae
Stem:	5—25 cm high, erect or ascending in a curve, slender, round, dark green, bristly hairs, several from one root
Leaves:	radical, rosettes, clustered, oblong-oval, singly to doubly pinnate, grey-green, hairy
Flowers:	terminal, solitary, erect, 40—60 mm diameter, five petals, obovate-round, some obtuse, golden yellow, pistil and numerous stamens also golden yellow; sepals shaped like a semi-basin, green, hairy outside
Flowering time:	July—August
Habitat:	2000—2700 m, calcareous and dolomite rock, screes, detritus, moraines. Rather rare.
Distribution:	Alps, Apennines, Pyrenees

PROTECTED!

CARNIOLAN GROUNDSEL

Senecio carniolicus

Family: Daisy Family Compositae

Stem: 5—20 cm high, towering, grey downy, sparsely foliate, green with grey shimmer

Leaves: radical, rosettes, obovate, crenate to pinnately lobed, downy, seldom bare, green with grey shimmer, stem leaves spatulate, pinnately lobed with narrow lobes, green — grey downy, stalked

Flowers: terminal umbels or clusters, several flowerheads, golden yellow, up to 1.5 cm large, flower bracts only slightly crenate, green-grey

Flowering time: July—October

Habitat: 1700—3200 m, soils deficient in lime, siliceous rock, recesses in the rock, moraines, screes, mountain ridges. Quite frequent.

Distribution: eastern Alps

SHRUBBY MILKWORT

Polygala chamaebuxus

Family: Milkwort Family Polygalaceae

Stem: 5—25 cm long, prostrate, creeping or ascending, branching, runners, round, strong, green-brown, some woody, foliate (small subshrub)

Leaves: alternate, sessile, ovate, blunt, tapering into stalk, entire, shiny above, leathery, evergreen

Flowers: terminal, clustered or emerging from upper leaf axils, whitish yellow erect wings; keel four-lobed, bright yellow or purple

Flowering time: February—August (some as from November)

Habitat: 600—2500 m, calcareous, poor soils, rocks, meadows, pastures, dry turf, open fir woods, amongst Alpine roses and pines.
Frequent, gregarious.

Distribution: Alps, Apennines, Pyrenees, Jura, Carpathians

ALPINE AVENS

Geum montanum

Family: Rose Family Rosaceae

Stem: 5—30 cm high, erect, strong, round, green-brown, foliate, hairy, no runners

Leaves: radical, rosettes, very large, oblong-spatulate, pinnate, reniform, lobed end leaf, lobes deeply notched, green, hairy, stalked; stem leaflets three or five-lobed, wide-lanceolate, hairy, alternate, sessile

Flowers: terminal, solitary, 25—50 mm diameter, five to six petals, ovate-round, some margined, golden yellow; stamens and style somewhat darker yellow; fruit a tuft of twisted, hairy styles, brown-red, serving as wings for the seeds. Calyx with several points, lanceolate, green, accumbent, hairy

Flowering time: July—August

Habitat: 1700—3200 m, siliceous and shaly soils, sunny mountain meadows, strips of rock, by Alpine roses, stony slopes, boulders.
Scattered.

Distribution: Alps, Apennines, Pyrenees

CREEPING AVENS

Geum reptans

Family:	Rose Family Rosaceae
Stem:	5—20 cm high, prostrate or ascending, foliate, reddish brown like the long runners, hairy
Leaves:	rosettes, pinnate, leaflet notched, dark green, shiny, hairy beneath, stalked
Flowers:	terminal, usually seven petals, obovate, golden yellow, slightly notched, entire; numerous stamens, sometimes a darker yellow, five sepals, pointed, brown-green, hairy; fruit bright red-brown, fluffily curling tufts act as wings for the seeds
Flowering time:	July—August
Habitat:	1800—3200 m, soils deficient in lime, rocky ridges, screes, moraines, boulders. Rather rare.
Distribution:	Alps

COWSLIP

Primula veris

Family: Primrose Family Primulaceae

Stem: 8—35 cm high, erect, strong, round, yellow-green, slightly hairy, leafless

Leaves: radical, rosettes, oblong ovate, with wide, flat stalk, notched, crinkled, mignonette green, hairy young leaves turned back

Flowers: terminal, one-sided umbel, corolla funnel-shaped, five petals, inversely cordate, notched, golden yellow, orange throat, spotted; calyx long, inflated, green, stalked, hairy

Flowering time: March—May

Habitat: 800—2200 m, sunny, warm soils, mountain meadows, pastures, open deciduous and mixed woodland, sunny slopes, stony hillsides.
Infrequent, gregarious.

Distribution: Alps, Apennines, Pyrenees

YELLOW OX—EYE

Bupthalmum salicifolium

Family: Daisy Family Compositae

Stem: 20—60 cm high, erect or ascending, branching, green, round, foliate, bush-shaped plant

Leaves: radical, stalked, cordate to wide lance-olate, serrate-crenate, green; stem leaves lanceolate, sessile, some encircling stalk, toothed, ciliate

Flowers: terminal on the shoots, corolla 4—6 cm in diameter, outside ray florets, linear, blunt, toothed, golden yellow; inside disc florets, glandular, golden yellow; sepals very small, lanceolate, green, accumbent

Flowering time: July—September

Habitat: 800—2000 m, soils rich in humus, stony turf, mountain meadows, banks of streams, warm slopes, ridges of rock. Quite frequent.

Distribution: Alps, northern Apennines

MOSSY SAXIFRAGE
Saxifraga bryoides

Family: Saxifrage Family Saxifragaceae
Cushion plant, moss-like, dense, green, little stems up to 6 cm high, round, slender, brownish red

Leaves: basal leaves linear-lanceolate, pointed, ciliate at edge, moss-like, rosettes, green, very small, stem leaves small, accumbent, inconspicuous, green-brown

Flowers: terminal, single flowers, five petals 4—6 mm long, elliptical-pointed, star-shaped, cream coloured, darker beige on ground, ten stamens, protruding, calyx in spiny points

Flowering time: July—August

Habitat: 1900—4000 m, siliceous and shaly detritus, glacial moraines, crevices, screes

Distribution: Alps, Pyrenees, Carpathians, Balkans

Note: Saxifraga bryoides is one of the Alpine flowering plants found at the highest altitudes (up to 4200 m)

ENTIRELY PROTECTED!

HEARTSEASE
Viola tricolor

Family:	Violet Family Violaceae
Stem:	8—20 cm long, prostrate or ascending, branching, angular, foliate, slender, hairy, green
Flowers:	terminal, solitary, large, 2.5—5 cm in diameter, five petals, spreading, obovate, yellowish white — light violet (tricoloured), marked with dark red lines towards base, spur short, blunt; five sepals, lanceolate, 20—30 mm long, green, accumbent
Leaves:	alternate, ovate-lanceolate, long, pointed, green; stipules lanceolate, pinnate, green
Flowering time:	June—August (September)
Habitat:	up to 2400 m, calcareous, poor soils, edges of fields, embankments, walls, fine detritus, cornfields, potato fields, screes. Scattered, gregarious.
Distribution:	Alps, Apennines, Pyrenees, Norway

GLOBEFLOWER

Trollius europaeus

Family:	Buttercup Family Ranunculaceae
Stem:	10—70 cm high, erect, slender, round, sometimes branching, green, bare, foliate
Leaves:	radical, long stalked, palmate, deeply cut, crenate-serrate, green, slightly hairy; stem leaves sessile, five or three merous, lobes lanceolate, serrate, green
Flowers:	terminal, spherical head, 20—40 mm diameter, up to fifteen almost round petals in a depressed globe, golden yellow, narrow stamens and nectary inside
Flowering time:	June—July
Habitat:	700—2400 m, damp meadows, grassy ridges, mountain pastures, banks of streams. Quite frequent.
Distribution:	Alps, Apennines, Pyrenees, Norway

Field of flowers near Namlos, Lechtal Alps, Tyrol

ALPINE COLUMBINE

Aquilegia alpina

Family: Buttercup Family Ranunculaceae

Stem: 20—65 cm high, ramose, round, strong, green, red tinged, bare, foliate

Leaves: radical leaves stalked, double trifoliate, crenate, deeply cut, dark green; stem leaves sessile, secondary leaflets trifoliae, narrow-lanceolate, sessile

Flowers: long-stalked, nodding, large, 4—8 cm in diameter, five sepals, ovate, pointed, five long spurs hooked at end, five ovate petals — round, bright blue, bracts projecting, golden yellow stamens, protruding

Flowering time: July—August

Habitat: 1200—2500 m, loose soils, meadows, open woods, edge of woods, clearings, bushes, wetlands, pastures.
Not frequent.

Distribution: Alps, northern Apennines

PROTECTED!

ALPINE ASTER

Aster alpinus

Family:	Daisy Family Compositae
Stem:	10—25 cm high, erect, foliate, green, round, pubescent
Leaves:	radical, stalked, spatulate, green, central vein, stem leaflets lanceolate, sessile, green
Flowers:	terminal, single head, one row of ray florets, linear, violet to pink; disc florets yellow; bracts green, several rows, accumbent
Flowering time:	June—August
Habitat:	1000—2600 m, dry, sunny soils, stony, overgrown slopes, rocky ridges, pastures, crevices. Quite frequent.
Distribution:	Alps, Pyrenees, Apennines

TRUMPET GENTIAN

Gentiana kochiana

Family: Gentian Family Gentianaceae

Stem: 2—5 cm long, erect or prostrate, green-brownish, strong, foliate

Leaves: radical, rosettes, wide-elliptic, herbaceous, blunt, soft, shiny, grass green; ovate stem leaflets in one or two pairs

Flowers: terminal, solitary, large, 5—7 cm long, flowers in trumpets, five points, spreading, bright white, tinged a delicate olive green outside, olive green spotting inside, white connecting membrane in the wide indentations between the petals, 5 stamens, whitish style and stigma, sepal teeth projecting

Flowering time: May—August

Habitat: 1400—2800 m, grassy slopes, screes, mountain meadows, pastures. Quite frequent.

Distribution: Alps, Pyrenees, Apennines, Apuan Alps

PROTECTED!

SPRING GENTIAN
Gentiana verna

Family: Gentian Family Gentianaceae

Stem: 3—8 cm high, erect, round, green, foliate

Leaves: radical, rosettes, elliptic-lanceolate, entire, green, different lengths; stem leaflets opposite, small-lanceolate, decurrent

Flowers: terminal, solitary, corolla spread out flat, approx. 25 mm diameter, five petal lobes, wide lanceolate or ovate, azure, throat whitish, ciliate; calyx tubular, green-blue outside; sepals lanceolate, long, pointed, green

Flowering time: March—July

Habitat: 800—3000 m, calcareous and siliceous rock, meadows, sunny pastures, boulders, alps, rocky ledges.
Quite frequent.

Distribution: Alps, Pyrenees, Abruzzi

BLADDER GENTIAN

Gentiana ultriculosa

Family:	Gentian Family Gentianaceae
Stem:	12—25 cm high, erect, angular, branching, green-brown, foliate, bare
Leaves:	rosettes, obovate, blunt, green; stem leaflets in pairs, long-lanceolate, sessile, green
Flowers:	one-sided, stalked, 5 lobes, spreading, 15—25 mm diameter, azure blue, tube whitish inside; calyx very long, narrow, broad wings, stalk emerging from pair of opposite leaves
Flowering time:	May—August
Habitat:	800—2200 m, stony, sandy soils, pastures, meadows, wetlands, screes, bogs. Not frequent, rare in places.
Distribution:	Alps

COMMON MONKSHOOD

Aconitum napellus

Family:	Buttercup Family Ranunculaceae
Stem:	40—140 cm high, erect, strong, round to angular, green to brown, foliate, hollow
Leaves:	alternate, palmate, cut to the middle in five to seven sections, crenate, green, lower leaves stalked, upper leaves sessile
Flowers:	long spike-like raceme, five petals, top one helmet-like, deep blue, two stalked nectaries and numerous white stamens protruding from corolla
Flowering time:	July—September
Habitat:	900—2700 m, nutritious soils, alpine pastures, crevices, overgrown ridges. Quite frequent.
Distribution:	Alps, Pyrenees
Note:	entire plant extremely poisonous.

PROTECTED!

DOLOMITES BELLFLOWER

Campanula morettiana

Family: Bellflower Family Campanulaceae

Stem: 1—6 cm long, hanging or ascending, round, green, stiff hairs, foliate, several from one root

Leaves: wide-oval to round, toothed, green, stiff hairs, lower leaves stalked, upper leaves sessile

Flowers: terminal, solitary, 1.5—2.5 cm diameter, funnel-shaped — bell-shaped, five petals, blue violet to red violet, hairy; calyx accumbent, very small, green, five sepals; stamens yellow

Flowering time: August—October

Habitat: 1500—2400 m, calcareous and dolomite rock, in the finest cracks and crevices, in more exposed places than edelweiss and wormwood.
Rare.

Distribution: Alps (Dolomites from the South Tyrol to Venetia)

PROTECTED!

MOUNT CENIS BELLFLOWER

Campanula cenisia

Family: Bellflower Family Campanulaceae

Stem: 3—25 cm long, sprawling, prostrate, round, slender, bare, green, foliate

Leaves: rosettes, ovate — round, entire, fleshy, green, ciliate; stem leaves wide-lanceolate, opposite, sessile, smaller, green, shiny

Flowers: on short stalks, terminal, solitary, bells, angular, corolla five-lobed, deeply cut, steel blue to slate grey, spreading, corolla diameter 15—25 mm, pistil and stamens yellow, calyx with five sepals, lanceolate, green, rough hairs, accumbent

Flowering time: July—September

Habitat: 2000—2900 m, shaly and calcareous rocks, screes, detritus, ridges. Very rare.

Distribution: Alps (western Alps) eastwards as far as the Lechtaler Alps

CREEPING BELLFLOWER

Campanula rapunculoides

Family:	Bellflower Family Campanulaceae
Stem:	15—80 cm high, erect, slender, round, green-brown, foliate, slightly hairy
Leaves:	alternate, sessile, ovate-lanceolate-oblong, dark green, crenate, reticulate, upper stem leaflets narrow, pointed, lower ones long-stalked, ovate-triangular
Flowers:	one-sided spike, numerous flowers, short stalked, funnel-shaped-campanulate, five petals curved backwards, nodding, up to 3.5 cm long and 3 cm diameter, light violet to dark blue-mauve, less frequently white, ciliate, five stamens, whitish
Flowering time:	June—September
Habitat:	600—1700 m, various soils, stony meadows, pastures, banks. Scattered, gregarious, prolific locally.
Distribution:	Alps, Apennines

BEARDED BELLFLOWER

Campanula barbata

Family: Bellflower Family Campanulaceae

Stem: 10—35 cm high, erect, strong, round, foliate, hairy

Leaves: radical, oblong-spatulate, entire, green, hairy; stem leaves smaller, lanceolate, green, sessile, entire, hairy on both sides

Flowers: one-sided raceme, nodding, stalked, ventricose-campanulate, five points, pale blue to mauve, some white, five epicalyx sepals, hairy, five calyx sepals, accumbent, pointed, green

Flowering time: June—August

Habitat: 1500—2500 m, poor soils, deficient in lime, mountain meadows, pastures, often gregarious with arnica. Frequent.

Distribution: Alps, Norway

CLUSTERED BELLFLOWER

Campanula glomerata

Family:	Bellflower Family Campanulaceae
Stem:	25—50 cm high, erect, strong, angular, foliate, slightly hairy, green, brown tinged
Leaves:	radical, stalked, cordate, slightly serrate; stem leaves oblong to lanceolate, alternate, sessile, crenate-serrate; bracts smaller, just beneath flower cluster, green, irregularly serrate
Flowers:	terminal, clustered, some in upper leaf axils, corolla funnel to bell-shaped, five petals, blue-violet, 1.5—2.5 cm diameter, 1.5—3 cm long, erect, five stamens, white
Flowering time:	June—August
Habitat:	800—1700 m, poor soils, mountain meadows, overgrown stony ground and slopes, pastures. Scattered.
Distribution:	Alps, Jura

PEACH—LEAVED BELLFLOWER

Campanula persicifolia

Family:	Bellflower Family Campanulaceae
Stem:	30—100 cm high, erect, round, slender, green, sometimes reddish brown above, foliate, bare
Leaves:	lower leaves oblong-ovate, tapering to stem, entire, upper stem leaves sessile, lanceolate to linear, light green, margin slightly serrate
Flowers:	loose racemes, short stalks, broad bells, 2.5—4 cm diameter, five petals, wide-ovate, pointed, light violet to light blue, nodding, edge turned back; stigma three-merous, whitish yellow, five dark yellow stamens, five-merous calyx, lobes short, green, accumbent
Flowering time:	May—August
Habitat:	up to 2000 m, poor soils, sunny meadows, open woods, bushes, edge of woods, mountain fields, warm slopes, clearings. Scattered, gregarious, locally prolific.
Distribution:	Alps

SCHEUCHZER'S HAREBELL

Campanula scheuchzeri

Family:	Bellflower Family Campanulaceae
Stem:	8—30 cm high, erect or ascending, sometimes crooked, slender, green, foliate, slightly hairy
Leaves:	radical leaves rounded, long-stalked, notched, dark green; stem leaves alternate, oblong-linear, upper leaves narrowly lanceolate, acicular, entire
Flowers:	mainly solitary, terminal, erect, bell-shaped, 20—25 mm diameter, 20—35 mm long, corolla with five petals, slightly turned back, blue-violet; sepals narrow-acicular, turning out, green; five stamens, yellow to white
Flowering time:	July—September
Habitat:	800—3000 m, nutritious soils deficient in lime, mountain meadows, pastures, rocky strips, overgrown ridges, stony slopes, edge of woods, overgrown screes. Scattered, gregarious.
Distribution:	Alps, Pyrenees

NETTLE-LEAVED BELLFLOWER

Campanula trachelium

Family:	Bellflower Family Campanulaceae
Stem:	25—90 cm high, erect, strong, angular, reddish brown, hairy, branching, foliate
Leaves:	alternate, wide-lanceolate, toothed, green, hairy, lower leaves stalked, nettle-like
Flowers:	loose, one-sided raceme, flowers large, 3—5 cm long, 2—3 cm diameter, bells, corolla with five petals, light blue-violet, more rarely white, margin ciliate, style thin, stigma three-merous, whitish
Flowering time:	July—August
Habitat:	900—2000 m, stony, loose loamy soils, sunny or semi-shaded meadows, edge of woods, pastures. Rather rare, gregarious.
Distribution:	Alps, Pyrenees

KING OF THE ALPS

Eritrichium nanum

Family:	Borage Family Boraginaceae
Stem:	up to 4 cm high, erect, round, slender, foliate, green; forming cushions or loose turf
Leaves:	in rosettes, lanceolate-spatulate, 6—12 mm long, 2—5 mm wide, green-grey, rough hairs, sessile; numerous rosettes forming small cushions
Flowers:	solitary, more rarely several on one stalk, terminal, very small, 4—8 mm in diameter, petals obovate to round, flat spreading, sky blue, yellow throat; calyx very small, five-merous, florets with bracts, green
Flowering time:	July—September
Habitat:	2500—3400 m, on dolomite and siliceous rock, fine screes, snowy valleys, crevices, ridges, moraines, near glaciers and defying extremes of weather. Rare.
Distribution:	Alps, Carpathians, Caucasus (central Alps and Dolomites).

PROTECTED!

COMMON PASQUE FLOWER

Pulsatilla vulgaris

Family:	Buttercup Family Ranunculaceae
Stem:	6—35 cm high, erect, strong, green-grey, hairy, foliate
Leaves:	radical leaves rosette-like, long stalked, 2-pinnate and 3-pinnate, narrow-linear tips, pointed, green, hairy, appearing after flowering; top leaves whorled, approx. half-way up stem, pointing outwards, fluffy hairs
Flowers:	solitary, large, 6 sepals, 3—4 cm long, oblong-ovate, light violet, hairy outside, bell-shaped, tips turned back, numerous ovaries with long violet stigmas surrounded by numerous golden stamens
Flowering time:	March—May
Habitat:	800—1700 m, calcareous, stony soils, meadows, stony slopes. Rather rare.
Distribution:	Alps, Jura, Pyrenees, Apennines

COMPLETELY PROTECTED! POISONOUS!

ALPINE ERYNGO or QUEEN OF THE ALPS

Eryngium alpinum

Family: Carrot Family Umbelliferae

Stem: 40—100 cm high, erect, one to several heads, bare, sulcate, green to light brown, foliate

Leaves: stem leaves at top three-lobed to palmately lobed, sessile, bluish, basal leaves oval-triangular, dentate-serrate, stalked

Flowers: umbel of many amethyst blue florets surrounded by light blue tinged, spiny bracts which open in the sun

Flowering time: July—September

Habitat: 1200—2400 m, calcareous soils, stony pastures, meadows, by dwarf pines, nutritious land, sheltered from wind, slopes.

Distribution: Alps, predominantly western Alps

COMPLETELY PROTECTED!

STICKY PRIMROSE
Primula glutinosa

Family:	Primrose Family Primulaceae
Stem:	2—8 cm high, erect, slender, round, greenish brown, glandular, leafless
Leaves:	radical, lanceolate-cuneate, rather fleshy, toothed, green
Flowers:	one to seven in an umbel, five petals, 10—15 mm diameter, petal lobes deeply notched, violet — violet pink, throat whitish, glandular hairs with darker eye, fragrant. Calyx accumbent, brown to dark red, scaly
Flowering time:	July—August
Habitat:	1800—3000 m, neutral to acid soils, siliceous rock, overgrown ridges, stony pastures, snowy valleys, screes. Frequent, scattered, prolific locally.

Distribution: Alps (central Alps)

PROTECTED!

ALPINE SNOWBELL

Soldanella alpina

Family:	Primrose Family Primulaceae
Stem:	5—15 cm high, erect or ascending in a curve, round, slender, brown-red, bare, leafless, curved at top
Leaves:	radical, stalked, reniform-round, small, entire, green, matt-shiny, cut at base, matt green beneath
Flowers:	one to three on stem, funnel to bell-shaped, deeply fringed, blue-violet, more rarely white, nodding; five sepals, lanceolate, turned outwards, green-brown, pistil protruding, long-pointed
Flowering time:	April—August (depending on when snow melts)
Habitat:	1200—2800 m, calcareous, damp soils, loamy pastures, mountain meadows, snowy valleys. Quite frequent, prolific locally.
Distribution:	Alps, Apennines, Pyrenees

DWARF SNOWBELL
Soldanella pusilla

Family: Primrose Family Primulaceae

Stem: 3—10 cm high, erect, round, slender, reddish brown, leafless, nodding

Leaves: basal rosettes, short-stalked, reniform, round, entire, green, prominent ribs, shiny, smaller than in Alpine Snowbell

Flowers: solitary, nodding, tubular bells, 9—16 mm long, shallow fringe, violet to pink, dark red stripes inside; five sepals, lanceolate, accumbent, violet

Flowering time: May—August

Habitat: 1500—3000 m, damp soils deficient in lime, overgrown ridges, mountain meadows, snowy valleys, pastures. Infrequent.

Distribution: Alps, north-west Apennines

ALPINE PANSY

Viola alpina

Family:	Violet Family Violaceae
Stem:	2—4 cm high, erect or ascending, round, slender, green, several from one branching root
Leaves:	radical, rosettes, small, ovate, notched, green; stipules growing into leaf stalk
Flowers:	terminal, solitary, conspicuously large, 30—40 mm diameter, petals spreading, obovate, deep violet, darker veins, throat light yellow, spur slightly up-turned
Flowering time:	June—October
Habitat:	1500—2400 m, calcareous soils, stony meadows, banks of streams, pastures, ridges, screes, boulders. Not frequent, gregarious.
Distribution:	Alps, Carpathians (northern limestone Alps, more rarely central Alps)

ROUND-HEADED RAMPION

Phyteuma orbiculare

Family:	Bellflower Family Campanulaceae
Stem:	15—50 cm high, erect or ascending, round, green-brown, weakly foliate
Leaves:	basal rosettes, long-pointed, notched-serrate, lower leaves stalked, bare, green
Flowers:	terminal, solitary, globular heads, deep blue — violet, petals turned inwards like claws, sometimes spiral appendages at tip; bracts lanceolate, narrow, pointed, green
Flowering time:	May—September
Habitat:	800—2600 m, loamy, warm soils, meadows, pastures, wetlands, clearings, screes. Quite frequent.
Distribution:	Alps, Apennines, Pyrenees

WOOD SCABIOUS

Knautia dipsacifolia (= Scabiosa sylvatica)

Family: Scabious Family Dipsacaceae

Stem: 20—85 cm high, erect, strong, round, green, bare below, pubescent above, branching, foliate

Leaves: in pairs, opposite, sessile, wide-lanceolate, serrate-crenate, green, reticulate, hairy, undivided

Flowers: terminal, solitary on long stalks, heads 2.5—4 cm diameter, somewhat flattened, outmost florets larger than the inner ones, reddish violet, more rarely white, florets with five petals, four stamens, white or pink, calyx inconspicuous, green

Flowering time: June—September

Habitat: 400—2000 m, nutritious, loamy soils, edges of woods and bushes, clearings, gorges, banks of streams, mountain meadows.
Quite frequent, gregarious.

Distribution: Alps, Pyrenees

Daisies near the Tajaspitze, Lechtal Alps, Tyrol

ALPINE PASQUE FLOWER

Pulsatilla alpina

Family:	Buttercup Family Ranunculaceae
Stem:	15—50 cm high, erect, green, slightly hairy, foliate
Leaves:	radical, stalked, three in number, divided, pinnate, green, three pinnate leaf bracts
Flowers:	terminal, solitary, 6—7 cm large, usually 6 petals, pure white, flushed a delicate bluish purple outside, hairy, surrounding numerous golden yellow stamens
Fruit:	bearded tuft of many long-haired styles (winged)
Flowering time:	May—July
Habitat:	1500—2700 m, calcareous, mountain meadows, slopes, overgrown boulders, scrub, with alders. Not frequent.
Distribution:	Alps, Pyrenees, Apennines

PROTECTED!

EDELWEISS

Leontopodium alpinum

Family: Daisy Family Compositae

Stem: 5—20 cm high, erect or ascending, round, green, white woolly hairs, foliate, frequently several from one root

Leaves: basal rosettes, oblong-linear-lanceolate, green, entire, white woolly hairs; stem leaflets alternate, lanceolate-linear, sessile, blunt, strong woolly hairs

Flowers: in three to twelve small terminal heads, grey to yellowish brown, small, inconspicuous disc florets; flowerheads surrounded in star shape by lanceolate bracts, spreading, narrow, entire, different lengths, woolly white hairs

Flowering time: July—September

Habitat: 1800—3500 m, sunny, stony soils, rocks, crevices, high pastures, meadows, ridges.
Rather rare, locally gregarious.

Distribution: Alps, Apennines, Pyrenees

PROTECTED!

LLOYDIA or SNOWDON LILY

Lloydia serotina

Family:	Lily Family Liliaceae
Stem:	5—10 cm high, erect, slender, green-brown, foliate, bare
Leaves:	radical, frequently as long as the stem, narrow-linear, grassy, somewhat fleshy, green; usually two stem leaves, alternate, narrow-lanceolate, sessile, decurrent, light green
Flowers:	terminal, solitary, approx. 1.5 cm in diameter, erect, six petals, ovate-oblong, funnel-shaped, white with three reddish veins, slightly yellow-brown at base inside and outside; six light yellow stamens, somewhat longer than style
Flowering time:	July—August
Habitat:	2000—3000 m, humus, acid stony soils deficient in lime, damp spots in semi-shade, rocks, rocky strips, windy ridges, with dwarf shrubs, mossy grass. Isolated, absent in some areas.
Distribution:	Alps

WHITE FALSE HELLEBORINE

Veratrum album

Family: Lily Family Liliaceae

Stem: 40—140 cm high, erect, strong, green, foliate, hairy, branching above

Leaves: alternate, encircling stalk, very large, wide-lanceolate, parallel veined, green

Flowers: spiky on branches, too, short stalked, corolla with six petals, ovately pointed, spreading, greenish yellow to dull white, throat darker; calyx inconspicuous, stamens ochre yellow

Flowering time: July—August

Habitat: 800—2700 m, damp, loamy soils, pastures, meadows.
Frequent.

Distribution: Alps

Note: entire plant extremely poisonous, mere contact leads to symptoms of poisoning.

BURNT ORCHID

Orchis ustulata

Family: Orchid Family Orchidaceae

Stem: 8—25 cm high, erect, strong, round, green, not branching, weakly foliate

Leaves: radical, ovate, wide, pointed, grass green, somewhat fleshy, parallel veined; stem leaves lanceolate, sessile or decurrent, unspotted, keeled

Flowers: dense conical spikes or rounded-off cylinders, florets 8—12 mm long, upper petals in a close helmet, three-lobed lip, side lobes projecting, central lobe long, white, notched, dark red spots, spur blunt, short, pointing down; top of spike seemingly dark purple due to buds, fragrant.

Flowering time: May—June

Habitat: 800—2000 m, calcareous soils, warm meadows, pastures, mountain fields. Infrequent.

Distribution: Alps, Apennines, Pyrenees

PROTECTED!

197

WHITE CROCUS

Crocus albiflorus

Family:	Iris Family Iridaceae
Stem:	mock pedicel, tubular, joining petals to corm, 6—12 cm high, erect, white, mauve or violet, bare
Leaves:	emerging from the corm, the leaves surround the flower stalk, narrow-linear, grass-like, green with central white stripe, keeled, developing after flowering
Flowers:	solitary, erect, large, bell-shaped, six petals, spatulate, entire, white, mauve or violet, tapering downwards into a tubular stalk, three stamens, golden yellow, style three-lobed, orange to yellowish red; ovary beneath ground in spring, above in summer
Flowering time:	March—June (depending on snow conditions and altitude)
Habitat:	700—2700 m, soils rich in humus, fields, mountain meadows, pastures. Very frequent, gregarious, very prolific locally.
Distribution:	Alps, Apennines, Pyrenees, Jura, Carpathians, Balkans

SPRING PASQUE FLOWER

Pulsatilla vernalis

Family:	Buttercup Family Ranunculaceae
Stem:	up to 15 cm high, erect or ascending, strong, green, round, golden, furry, hairy, foliate
Leaves:	radical, rosette-like, stalked, palmate, pinnate, green, hairy; leaves under-developed or not yet present at flowering time. Three whorled bracts beneath flower, points long-linear, woolly hairs, green
Flowers:	solitary, terminal, ovate-campanulate, spreading when in full bloom to 40—60 mm diameter, six petals, obovate-round, white inside, outside pink to violet, furry hairs, numerous yellow stamens
Flowering time:	April—July
Habitat:	1000—3000 m, calcareous and siliceous soils, mountain meadows, pastures, fields and overgrown ridges. Somewhat rare.
Distribution:	Alps, Pyrenees, Norway

PROTECTED!

ST. BRUNO'S LILY
Paradisea liliastrum

Family:	Lily Family Liliaceae
Stem:	30—50 cm high, erect, strong, round, leafless, bare, unbranching, green
Leaves:	radical, almost as long as the stem, narrow, grass-like, green, standing erect, not grooved
Flowers:	one-sided racemes, few in flower at same time, funnel-shaped, large, approx. 5 cm diameter, long petal points, pure white, on short stalks from leaf axils; small, lanceolate bracts, buds erect, flowers later nodding slightly; style somewhat longer than the six golden yellow stamens
Flowering time:	June—July
Habitat:	800—2400 m, calcareous, nutritious loamy soils, fond of warmth, on mountain fields, pastures, open bushes, stony slopes, with green elders. Gregarious, but rare and absent in many areas.
Distribution:	Alps, Pyrenees, Apennines (southern and northern limestone Alps)

SWISS ROCK-JASMINE

Androsace helvetica

Family:
Primrose Family Primulaceae
Dense, semi-spherical cushions, silvery grey — green, with small tile-like leafed branches, the plant grows very slowly and reaches an unusually great age, not infrequently up to 60 years.

Leaves:
tile-like on the tiny branches, rosettes, very small, green, dense woolly hairs, giving a silvery appearance

Flowers:
terminal, short stalked, flat spreading corolla out of the leaf axils, five petals, obovate, round, 4—6 mm in diameter, white with yellow eye, at the main flowering time the semi-spherical cushion is densely covered with florets

Flowering time:
May—July

Habitat:
1800—3500 m, calcareous soils, rocks, fine crevices; its marvellous adaptability enables this plant to survive many decades of severest weather conditions.
Scattered, absent in some areas of the eastern limestone Alps.

Distribution: Alps (north-west limestone Alps and Dolomites)

ENTIRELY PROTECTED!

STEMLESS CARLINE THISTLE

Carlina acaulis

Family: Daisy Family Asteraceae

Stem: 5—25 cm high, erect, prostrate or ascending, round, green, brownish red tinged, foliate

Leaves: rosettes, pinnate, spiny toothed, narrow, long, stiff, dark green, brownish red tinged at the base; lobes pinnate, extremely sharp

Flowers: terminal, single heads, flat flowerhead 6—12 cm large, tubular florets brownish above, whitish beneath, secreting nectar, surrounded by silvery white, narrow-lanceolate parchment-like bracts which open in the sun and close in the rain

Flowering time: July—September

Habitat: up to 2800 m, poor soils in meadows and pastures, sometimes in the grass, on calcareous, stony ground, open woodland, gregarious.
Quite frequent.

Distribution: Alps, Pyrenees, Apennines

PROTECTED!

MOUNTAIN AVENS

Dryas octopetala

Family:	Rose Family Rosaceae
Stem:	5—12 cm high, erect, slender, round, brown-red, glandular hairs
Leaves:	radical, stalked, lanceolate, notched, green, shiny above, silvery white downy beneath, length of leaf 3—6 cm, width of leaf 10—20 mm
Flowers:	solitary, terminal, flower diameter 3—5 cm, eight petals, ovate-oblong, blunt, white, numerous stamens, golden yellow
Flowering time:	May—August
Habitat:	800—2400 m, calcareous, stony soils, mountain meadows, detritus, overgrown boulders, wetlands, moraines, silted up areas, pioneer plant. Quite frequent, gregarious.
Distribution:	Alps, Apennines, Pyrenees, Norway

PANICULATE or LIVELONG SAXIFRAGE

Saxifraga paniculata

Family:	Saxifrage Family Saxifragaceae
Stem:	10—35 cm high, erect or ascending, round, ramose, slender, brownish red; weakly foliate, glandular hairy, sometimes cushion-like
Leaves:	rosettes, small, linear, blunt, toothed, green, lime encrusted at edges; stem leaves isolated, alternate, small, glandular, green
Flowers:	dense panicles, florets small, approx. 6—12 mm diameter, five petals, inversely spatulate, rayed out, yellowish white, some purple spotted; short, golden yellow stamens
Flowering time:	June—August
Habitat:	up to 3000 m, rocks, boulders, stony places, moraines. Quite frequent.
Distribution:	Alps, Pyrenees, Apennines

PROTECTED!

211

ALPINE MOON DAISY

Leucanthemopsis alpina

Family:	Daisy Family Compositae
Stem:	6—15 cm high, erect, green, slender, foliate, somewhat angular, turf-forming root
Leaves:	radical, stalked, deeply pinnate, lower stem leaves cuneate, three-toothed, green, upper leaves narrow-lanceolate, sessile, entire, slender
Flowers:	solitary, terminal, large 3—4 cm diameter, white, linear ray florets surrounding golden yellow disc florets, semi-spherical, green, dark edged bracts
Flowering time:	July—August
Habitat:	1800—3200 m, siliceous soils, shaly rock, fine detritus, moraines, snowy valleys, screes, pastures. In groups, but not frequent.
Distribution:	Alps, Pyrenees

Botany in brief

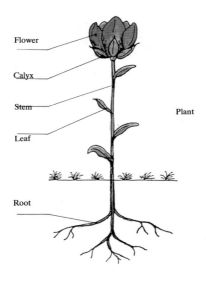

Flower

Calyx

Stem

Leaf

Plant

Root

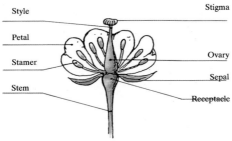

Style

Stigma

Petal

Stamer

Ovary

Sepal

Stem

Receptacle

STEM

branching

with knodes

angular

sulcate

erect

prostrate

ascending

PHYLLOTAXIS

rosette

alternate

opposite

verticillate
whorled

LEAF ARRANGEMENT

stalked

sessile

encircling stalk

— grooved

— decurrent

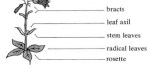
— bracts
— leaf axil
— stem leaves
— radical leaves
— rosette

LEAF FORMS

acicular

awl-shaped

lanceolate

linear

cuneate

spatulate

long

ovate

oblong-ovate

obovate

round

shield-shaped

rhomboidal

deltoid

reniform

cordate

inversely cordate

arrow-shaped

spear-shaped

palmately lobed

trifoliate

pinnately lobed

palmate

pedate

digitate

pinnate

unevenly pinnate

evenly pinnate

LEAF MARGINS

entire

serrate

doubly serrate

dentate, toothed

serrate-dentate

spiny-toothed

notched, crenate

sinuate

runcinate

VENATION

feathered

reticulate

parallel veined

CALYX

tubular

ventricose

dialysepalous

inflated

two-lipped

veined

epicalyx

with scale

217

INFLORESCENCES

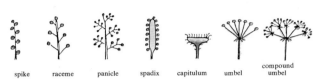

| spike | raceme | panicle | spadix | capitulum | umbel | compound umbel |

CYMES

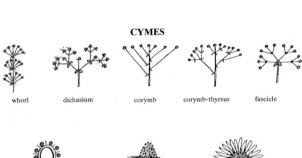

| whorl | dichasium | corymb | corymb-thyrsus | fascicle |

HÖHENSTUFEN DER ALPEN

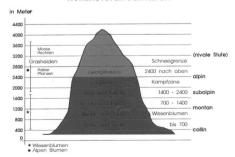

in Meter

4400		
4000		
3600	Moose Flechten	(nivale Stufe)
3200	Grasheiden	Schneegrenze
2800	Polster Pflanzen	
2400	Zwergstrauch	2400 nach oben · alpin
2000		Kampfzone
1600		1400 - 2400 subalpin
1200		700 - 1400 · montan
800		Wiesenblumen
400		bis 700 · collin
0		

★ Wiesenblumen
● Alpen Blumen

218